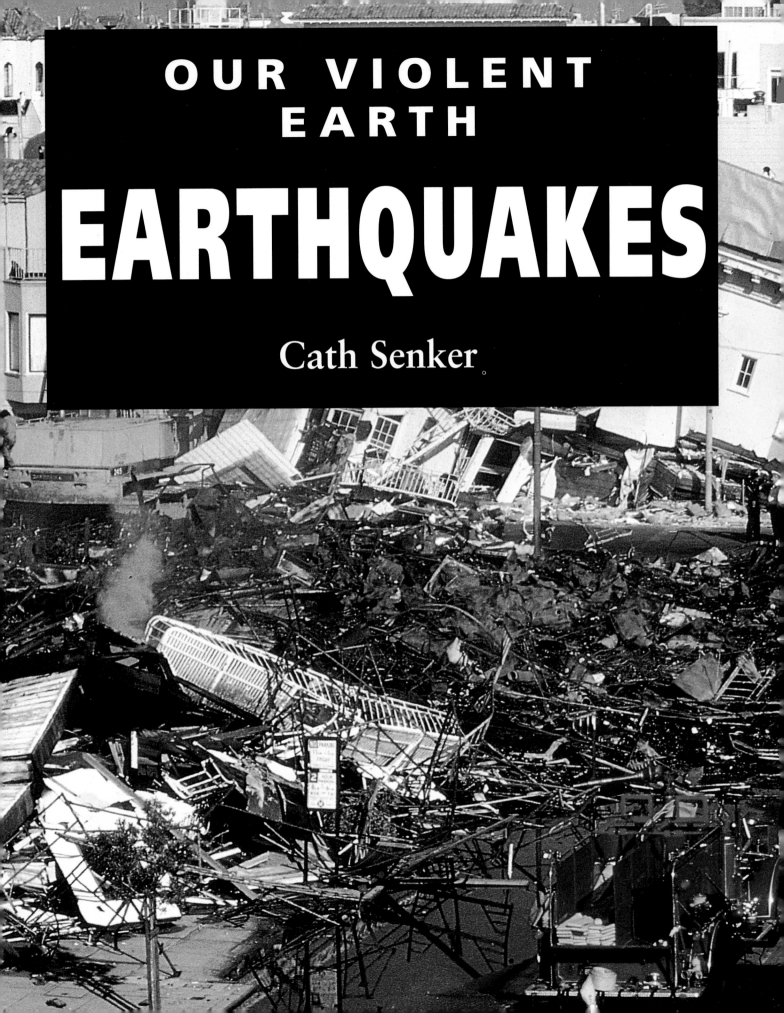

OUR VIOLENT EARTH

EARTHQUAKES

Cath Senker

OUR VIOLENT EARTH

EARTHQUAKES

Other titles in this series:
FLOODS ● STORMS ● VOLCANOES

Cover photograph: Rescue workers stand in the rubble of an earthquake in Turkey, in 1999.

Title page: Collapsed houses the day after the Loma Prieta earthquake in California, in October 1989.

Contents page: The San Andreas Fault crossing the Carrizo Plain in California.

This book is a simplified version of the title 'Earthquakes' in Hodder Wayland's 'Restless Planet' series.

Language level consultant: Norah Granger
Editor: Belinda Hollyer   Designer: Jane Hawkins

Text copyright © 2001 Hodder Wayland
Volume copyright © 2001 Hodder Wayland

First published in 2001 by Hodder Wayland,
an imprint of Hodder Children's Books.

British Library Cataloguing in Publication Data
Senker, Cath
Earthquakes. - (Our violent earth)
1.Earthquakes - Juvenile literature
I. Title
551.2'2
ISBN 0 7502 3509 8

Printed and bound in Italy by
G. Canale & C.S.p.A., Turin

Hodder Children's Books
A division of Hodder Headline Ltd
338 Euston Road, London NW1 3BH

Acknowledgements
The publishers would like to thank the following for allowing their photographs to be reproduced in this book: Camera Press 4, 18t, 26, 39; Robert Harding 40; Image Select/Ann Ronan 33; Impact 27; PHOTRI 22, 24; Popperfoto *Cover*, 5, 7, 18b, 19, 25, 35, 36, 37, 44, 45; Science Museum/Science & Society Picture Library 17; Science Photo Library *Title page*, 9, 20, 21, 38, 41, 42; Getty Images 28, 43.

Illustrations by Nick Hawken and Tim Mayer

Contents

Introducing Earthquakes   4

What Causes Earthquakes?   8

Measuring Earthquakes   16

The Dangers of Earthquakes   18

Earthquake Disasters   24

Tsunamis   32

Rescue and Relief Work   36

Preparing for Earthquakes   40

Glossary   46

Further Information   47

Index   48

Introducing Earthquakes

▲ Rescue workers looking for survivors in Armenia, in Colombia, January 1999.

A major earthquake is terrifying. On 17 August 1999, an earthquake hit north-western Turkey, killing 20,000 people. Many homes collapsed, burying those inside. Thousands of people were left homeless. Rescue teams could not reach many of the people trapped under the rubble.

NEWS REPORT

The tremor created a wave of destruction through twenty towns and villages in Colombia's mountainous coffee-growing area. "There are more than 1,000 dead, perhaps more than 2,000 in Armenia alone," said Ciro Antonio Guiza, the city's deputy fire chief.

Adapted from *The Guardian*, 27 January, 1999

Killer quakes

There are more than 3,000 earthquakes every year. A few cause serious damage. About 10,000 people are killed each year by earthquakes. But in some terrible cases many more die. In Tangshan City in China, in 1976, 240,000 people - the greatest number ever - were killed.

DID YOU KNOW ?

The longest earthquake yet recorded lasted four minutes, in Alaska, in 1964.

Studying earthquakes

Scientists cannot always tell when an earthquake will happen. Massive earthquakes can strike without warning. We will never be able to stop earthquakes. But if we can work out how to predict them, people can be warned to move away.

Huge damage

Major earthquakes destroy buildings, farmland and animals as well as killing people. After an earthquake, people may be left without basic things such as clean water, food and electricity. It can take years to rebuild towns and villages.

A survivor of the Kobe earthquake that hit Japan in January 1995. Over 2,000 people died. ▼

The after-effects of an earthquake

1. Death

Most people are killed by falling buildings.
But if buildings such as hospitals are destroyed,
many other people may die after the earthquake.

2. Injury and shock

Many people are injured, or are in shock from
losing friends and family.

3. Buildings destroyed

Buildings may be badly damaged. If buildings such
as hospitals are destroyed, important services
cannot run.

4. Economy breaks down

Shops, offices and factories may be closed down.
People lose their jobs and businesses.

5. Other natural disasters

Earthquakes can cause tsunamis (see page 32),
as well as landslides, mudflows and avalanches
(see page 22).

6. Animals and farms

Wild animals can lose their homes, and farmland
may be destroyed.

66 *EYEWITNESS* **99**

*"My children were
two steps behind me.
They died in each
other's arms."*

Catalina Valencia,
in Colombia, 1999

 **DID YOU
KNOW ?**

The world's most powerful
earthquake happened in
Chile in 1960. It measured
9.3 on the Richter scale,
which is more than
100,000 times more
powerful than a nuclear
explosion.

▲ People leaving the scene of the earthquake in Gibellina, in Sicily in January 1968.

This book tells how earthquakes and tsunamis are caused and why they are dangerous. It explains how studying the earth can help scientists to predict earthquakes better. Also, it shows how investigating the after-effects of earthquakes teaches us lessons for the future.

What Causes Earthquakes?

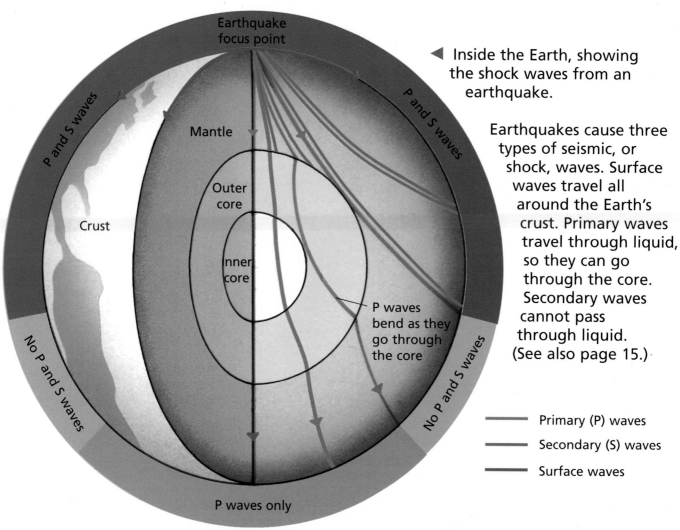

Earthquake focus point

P and S waves

Mantle

Outer core

Crust

Inner core

P waves bend as they go through the core

No P and S waves

P and S waves

No P and S waves

P waves only

 Inside the Earth, showing the shock waves from an earthquake.

Earthquakes cause three types of seismic, or shock, waves. Surface waves travel all around the Earth's crust. Primary waves travel through liquid, so they can go through the core. Secondary waves cannot pass through liquid. (See also page 15.)

—— Primary (P) waves

—— Secondary (S) waves

—— Surface waves

Inside the Earth

The Earth is made up of three main layers. In the centre is the core. Around the core is the mantle, a thick layer of rock. The mantle is mainly solid, but is molten (liquid) close to the surface. The outer layer is the crust, made up of huge slabs of rock called tectonic plates. Currents inside the mantle move the plates around the Earth.

DID YOU KNOW ?

The Earth is more than 4,550 million years old.

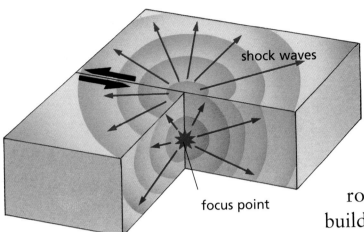

shock waves

focus point

This rock at the San Andreas Fault was twisted and folded as the tectonic plates moved beneath it. ▼

Plate movements

Tectonic plates travel in different directions at different speeds. They slide past each other with difficulty. Sometimes, one plate is forced under another. If moving rock becomes stuck, the pressure builds up until the rock suddenly tears apart. This causes an earthquake. The point where the rocks break is the focus point. From there, seismic waves spread out in all directions.

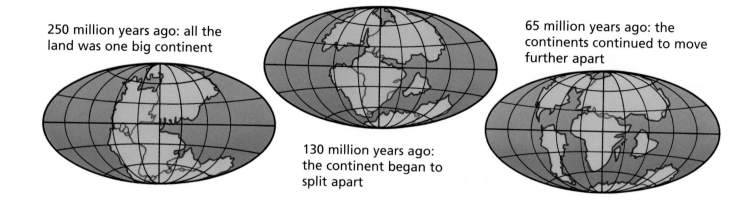

250 million years ago: all the land was one big continent

130 million years ago: the continent began to split apart

65 million years ago: the continents continued to move further apart

▲ The super-continent broke up over millions of years. Alfred Wegener called the super-continent 'Pangaea'. It means 'all land'.

Continental drift

In 1915, a German scientist called Alfred Wegener suggested that millions of years ago, all the continents were joined together in one super-continent. He called it 'Pangaea'. Over millions of years, it broke up into separate continents, which continued to move apart. Alfred Wegener called this movement 'continental drift'.

DID YOU KNOW ?

Alfred Wegener worked out his idea of continental drift when he realized that the rocks and fossils of South America and South Africa were similar. He believed that they were once part of one continent. Scientists today agree with this idea.

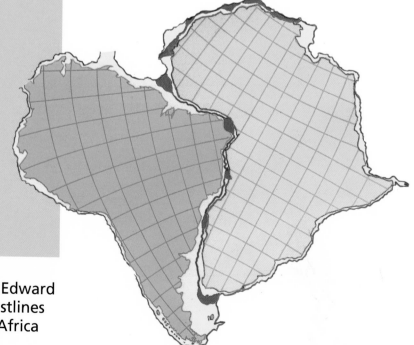

In 1965, a scientist called Sir Edward Bullard showed how the coastlines of South America (left) and Africa fit together. ▶

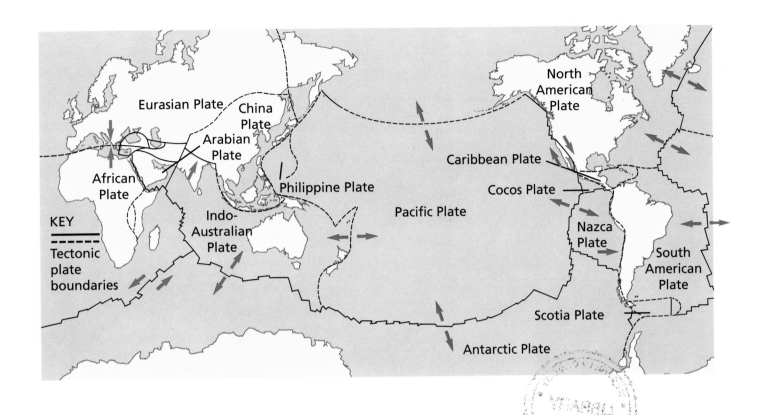

 This map shows the tectonic plates. The pink arrows show the direction the plates are moving in.

As the tectonic plates inside the Earth continue to move, continental drift continues too. The continents and oceans are still changing shape. Africa and North America are being slowly pushed apart, while the Pacific Ocean is shrinking. The Atlantic Ocean is getting bigger.

DID YOU KNOW ?

The world's continents move about 2 centimetres a year.

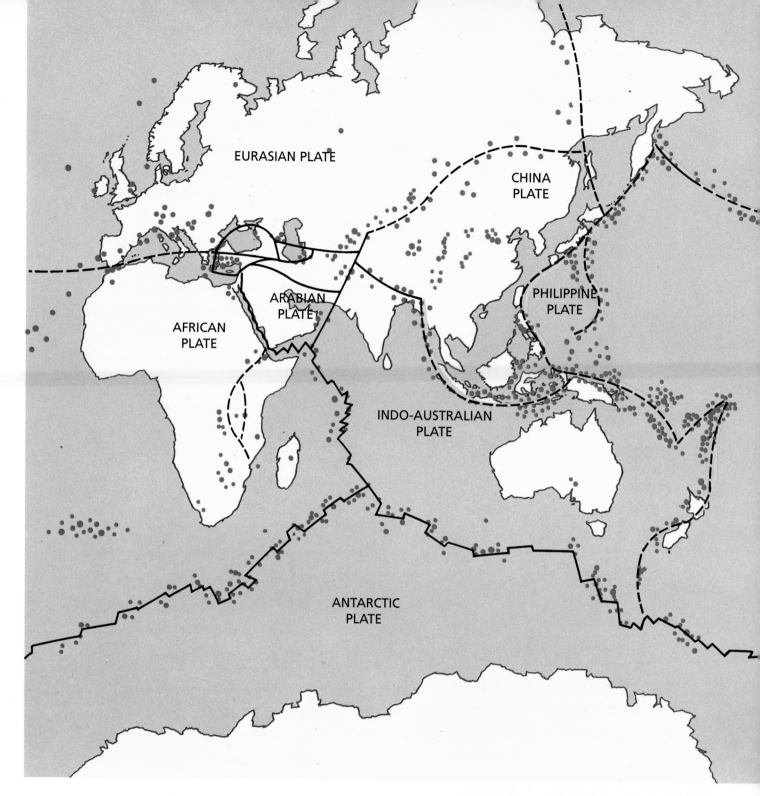

EURASIAN PLATE

CHINA PLATE

PHILIPPINE PLATE

ARABIAN PLATE

AFRICAN PLATE

INDO-AUSTRALIAN PLATE

ANTARCTIC PLATE

Subduction zones

Earthquakes occur when the edges of plates grind together. Sometimes one plate is pushed down beneath the other. This is called subduction. Areas where this happens are called subduction zones.

 DID YOU KNOW ?

About three-quarters of the world's earthquakes occur in the 'Ring of Fire'.

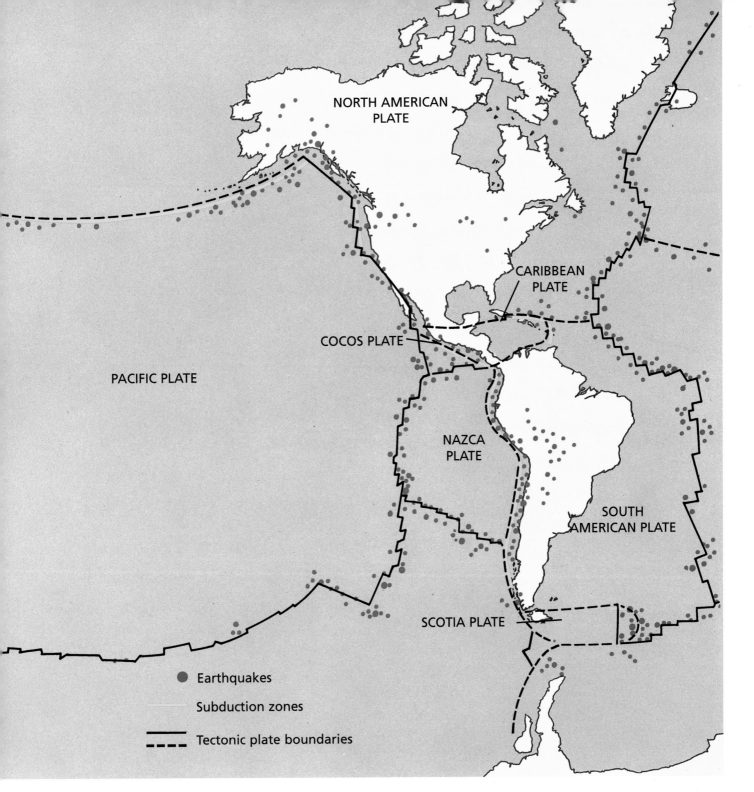

NORTH AMERICAN PLATE

CARIBBEAN PLATE

COCOS PLATE

PACIFIC PLATE

NAZCA PLATE

SOUTH AMERICAN PLATE

SCOTIA PLATE

- Earthquakes
— Subduction zones
---- Tectonic plate boundaries

The 'Ring of Fire'

The rim of the shrinking Pacific Ocean has the highest number of subduction zones. Earthquakes and volcanoes are very common here and it has been named the 'Ring of Fire'.

▲ The red dots on this map show where earthquakes happen.

How earthquakes happen

As the plates that make up the Earth's crust move and push together, the rocks sometimes crack. The places where they crack are called faults. The lines the cracks make are called fault lines. The world's biggest fault lines are near the edges of plates.

There is a 1,200-kilometre long fault between the Pacific and North American Plates in California, in the USA. It is called the San Andreas Fault. The rocks on either side of the fault do not move smoothly and often lock together. The stress in the rocks builds up until the rocks suddenly push past each other. This causes an earthquake.

How the land moves

The land can move in different ways during an earthquake, depending on which way the plates are travelling. The ground can move sideways, and also up and down.

The ground can move in different ways during an earthquake. ▼

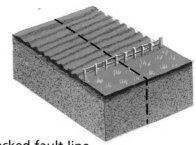

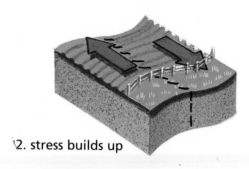

1. locked fault line

2. stress builds up

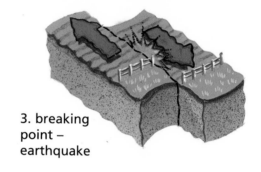

3. breaking point – earthquake

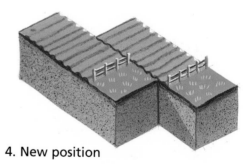

4. New position

▲ How rocks that are locked together along a fault line can cause an earthquake.

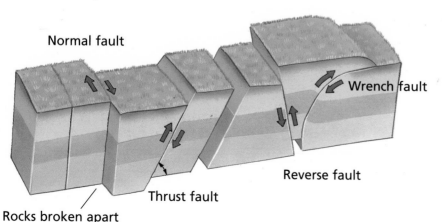

Normal fault

Wrench fault

Thrust fault

Reverse fault

Rocks broken apart

Seismic waves

During an earthquake, seismic waves move out from the focus point. They are strongest on the Earth's surface directly above the focus. This is the earthquake's epicentre.

TYPES OF SEISMIC WAVE

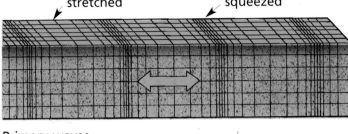

stretched   squeezed

Primary waves

◀ Body waves
Primary waves travel at about 6 kilometres per second. They make the rocks stretch and squeeze together, like a spring being stretched and let go.

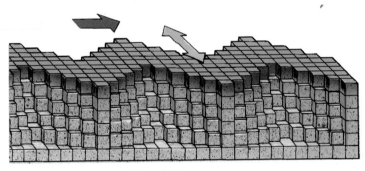

Secondary waves

◀ Secondary waves travel at about 3.5 kilometres a second. They make the rocks move up and down like ocean waves.

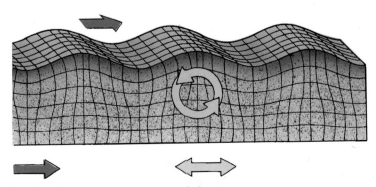

Love waves move side to side.

◀ Surface waves
Surface waves are slower than body waves but they cause more damage. This is partly because they take longer to pass through the rocks. There are two types: Love waves and Rayleigh waves.

Rayleigh waves move up and down.

Measuring Earthquakes

Measuring earthquakes

The scientists who study earthquakes are called seismologists. They use measuring instruments called seismometers to record the pattern of seismic waves. They can work out the strength of each earthquake, and how long it lasts. As seismic waves travel around and through the Earth, scientists can check on earthquakes from anywhere in the world. They can share information straight away on the internet.

EARTHQUAKE INSTRUMENTS

A strainmeter measures changing pressures on rocks.

A tiltmeter, placed underground, measures the rising or sinking of the ground.

A creepmeter measures the creep, or movement, of a fault.

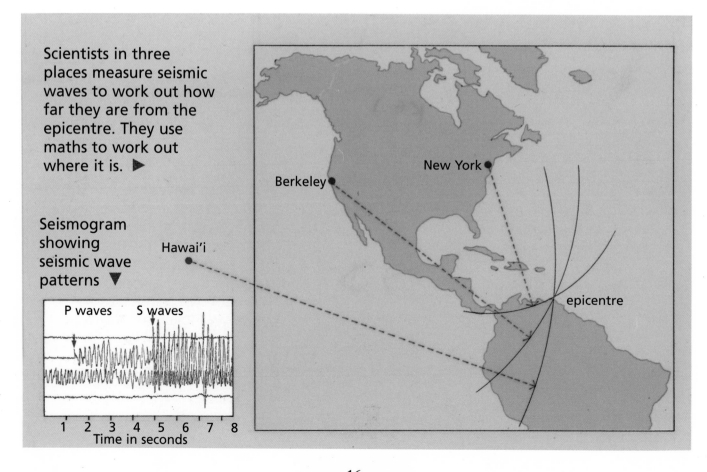

Scientists in three places measure seismic waves to work out how far they are from the epicentre. They use maths to work out where it is. ▶

Seismogram showing seismic wave patterns ▼

P waves   S waves

Time in seconds

Berkeley

New York

Hawai'i

epicentre

The Richter and Mercalli scales

Scientists use two scales to measure earthquakes. The Richter scale measures their size and strength. Each point on the scale means the earthquake is ten times stronger than the point below. The Mercalli scale measures how damaging earthquakes are.

In the year AD 132, a Chinese mathematician called Chang Heng invented this instrument to record earthquakes. When the ground moved, a ball fell from one of the dragon heads. ▶

The Richter and Mercalli scales

Richter	Mercalli	What happens
1–3	1	Not felt by people.
3–4	2–3	Felt by people at rest. Indoors, hanging objects may swing.
4–5	4–5	Felt by many indoors. Windows and objects rattle.
5–6	6–7	Felt by everyone; hard to stand up. Plaster and loose bricks fall; glass breaks.
6–7	8–9	People panic. Walls fall down; underground pipes break; the ground cracks. Weak buildings collapse.
7–9	10–12	Landslides; bridges are destroyed. Most buildings fall down. Wide cracks in ground. The ground moves in waves.

The Dangers of Earthquakes

Large earthquakes usually hit without warning. The ground may shake for about a minute, as the rocks along a fault line are smashed apart.

Huge damage

The ground movements cause terrible damage, especially in towns or cities. Roads may crack open, crushing cars and their passengers. Buildings can shake and collapse. Glass and bricks fly through the air. People rush out into the streets to escape falling houses, and are thrown to the ground.

▲ A rescue worker with sniffer dogs at the scene of the 1985 earthquake in Mexico.

▲ A victim is rescued after the 1995 earthquake in Neftegorsk, Russia.

 DID YOU KNOW ?
Earthquakes can cause the most damage if the focus point is less than 30 kilometres underground.

66 *EYEWITNESS* 99

"You didn't know whether to run or stand still; everything just came crashing down."

J. Delgano, Armenia,
in Colombia, 1999

The Hanshin highway collapsed during the earthquake in Kobe, in Japan, in 1995. ▼

Rescue

When the ground stops shaking, sirens and screams are heard. Fuel and power lines are broken, and fires may break out.

Rescuers look for survivors. Some are trapped under the rubble. The rescuers may have infra-red cameras to find people by their body heat. They may also use sniffer dogs. They have to hurry, because there may be after-shocks following the earthquake. Also, gas from broken gas pipes may catch fire.

Protection from earthquakes

People who are indoors during an earthquake should crouch in the doorway, or under a table.

The children of Parkfield School in California, in the USA, live on top of the San Andreas Fault. They are used to earthquakes. All desks and heavy equipment are bolted to the floor. Windows are criss-crossed with tape to stop broken glass flying through the air. The children practise their earthquake drill regularly. They crouch under the desks and cover their heads.

▲ Earthquake drill at Parkfield School in California.

66 *EYEWITNESS* 99

"...the earth started shaking... I could feel myself falling...The bedroom ceiling fell down on me."

Survivor in Golcuk in Turkey, 1999

Normal building   Earthquake-proof building

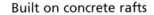

Built on solid foundations   Built on concrete rafts

▲ The earthquake-proof building moves on concrete rafts and can sway without falling.

TALL TOWERS

Tall buildings are the most likely to fall in a strong earthquake. In big cities, they are often close together. They sway and twist, sometimes knocking buildings around them and making them collapse, too.

Building rules

In many cities in earthquake zones, builders have to follow strict rules when they build or repair buildings. They strengthen the walls, floors, roofs and foundations. Special methods are used to make the buildings earthquake-proof. But these expensive methods are not used much in poor countries.

▲ Buildings without earthquake-proof foundations in Marina, in San Francisco, collapsed in the Loma Prieta earthquake in 1989.

Avalanches, Landslides and Mudflows

Earthquakes can cause other disasters, too.

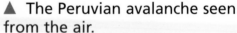

The Peruvian avalanche seen from the air.

Avalanches

In May 1970, there was an undersea earthquake in Peru. It measured 7.7 on the Richter scale. It was so strong that it caused part of the Huascarán mountain to collapse. A massive avalanche of snow and rock crashed down into the Rio Santo Valley.

Peru

The avalanche travelled at a terrifying 280 kilometres an hour as it hit the town of Yungay. In six minutes, the town was buried under 10 metres of rock. More than 50,000 people died.

DID YOU KNOW ?

Mining, dam-building and digging for oil put stress on rocks and can cause earthquakes.

NEWS REPORT

Two avalanches wiped out the town of Yungay after the earthquake in Peru on 31 May, 1970. Helicopter pilots estimated that 2,500 people took refuge on Yungay Cemetery Hill before the town was overwhelmed. Those...[people] were safe but unable to escape.

Adapted from the Press Association,
8 June 1970

Landslides

An earthquake can make a mass of rock and soil break away from a mountain. This can cause a landslide. In 1959, Madison Canyon in Montana, in the USA, was hit by a landslide after an earthquake. The earthquake measured 7.1 on the Richter scale. The landslide covered a camp-site, killing nineteen people. Shock waves also damaged the Hebgen Dam. It was a race against time to mend the dam before people living downstream were flooded out.

Mudflows

Heavy rain can cause rocks and soil loosened by an earthquake to flow downhill in a mudflow. Homes built on soft ground may fall over or sink in the mud. Mexico City is built on layers of mud, clay, gravel and sand. It suffered huge damage in the earthquake of 1985.

NEWS REPORT

Chamoli in northern India has been hit by a severe earthquake. A landslide covered 16 km of road leading to the worst-affected area. "It looks like half the mountain has come off," said the district magistrate, Uma Kant Pawar.

Adapted from Online BBC news,
30 March 1999

▲ A house tipped over by a landslide in Anchorage, in Alaska, in 1964.

Earthquake Disasters

Japan

Japan lies on a subduction zone in the Pacific Ocean, where two plates are diving down beneath another plate.

The Great Kanto Earthquake

On 1 September 1923, Japan was struck by a massive undersea earthquake. It measured 8.3 on the Richter scale. It was so powerful that it split the sea floor. The earthquake caused a tsunami too, as well as other after-shocks. Over half a million homes were destroyed in Tokyo and Yokohama, and 142,000 people died.

Fire

Many people were cooking lunch on open stoves when the earthquake struck. The stoves set fire to the wooden houses, and fires spread through Tokyo.

▲ Damage caused by the Great Kanto Earthquake, 1923.

▲ It is often hard to get clean drinking water after an earthquake.

FEWER DEATHS

"The number of deaths from earthquakes is now lower, probably because countries have made buildings safer."

a report by Dr Waverley Person, Director, National Earthquakes Information Center, in the USA

On this map, the areas hit by the Great Kanto Earthquake are shown in red. ▼

Japan

Kanto Plain

Tokyo

Yokohama

epicentre

Pacific Ocean

What we learned

Since the Great Kanto Earthquake, the Japanese have learnt how to prepare for earthquakes. Buildings are built in special ways to prevent earthquake damage. People have emergency kits with food, water and medicine. They practise earthquake drills.

In January 1995, an earthquake that measured 7.2 on the Richter scale hit the city of Kobe. About 6,000 people were killed, but more would have died if the city had not been prepared for an earthquake.

▲ Local people and soldiers used their bare hands to try to rescue people after the earthquake in Armenia.

Armenia

On 7 December 1988, an earthquake measuring 6.8 on the Richter scale struck Armenia. There had never been an earthquake there before, so people were not prepared for it. It is thought that between 25,000 to 100,000 people died.

Collapsed buildings

There was terrible damage to buildings. In Leninakan, where 290,000 people lived, 80 per cent of the buildings collapsed. In Spitak, the worst damage was to tower blocks built on ground that had been marshland before.

Since no one expected an earthquake, the buildings had not been strengthened to protect them. Many buildings were prefabricated – ready-made in sections – and the sections fell apart during the earthquake.

LIVING IN TOWNS

"More and more people live close together in towns, which makes the effects of earthquakes much worse."

Comments of Dr Waverley Person, Director, National Earthquakes Information Center, in the USA

ARMENIA

Caspian Sea

Black Sea

Spitak

Leninakan

Lake Sevan

 earthquake damage zone

◀ This map shows where the Armenian earthquake happened.

What we learned

Many people who were trapped died from their injuries, or from the cold. Others died from lack of air under the rubble.

Afterwards, people realized that more rescue teams, with proper equipment, should have been sent to the disaster area. They should have got there more quickly, too.

NEWS REPORT

Every spare hand carried out the frantic clear-up operation – life or death for the victims trapped beneath the rubble.

Adapted from Camera Press/TASS report, December 1988

Search and rescue

After the earthquake, many people were trapped under buildings that had collapsed. Local people organized search and rescue teams straight away. But the sixteen international aid teams did not arrive for another two days. Amazingly, some survivors were found nearly three weeks after the earthquake.

▲ Many died in damaged buildings like these.

California

The state of California in the USA lies on the boundary between two tectonic plates. The North American Plate is moving slowly southwards, but the Pacific Plate is moving north-west, much faster. This means there are fault lines all across California. It is a major earthquake zone.

The most famous fault is the San Andreas Fault. In 1999, seismologists discovered a fault lying under Los Angeles. They believe this fault could cause the biggest earthquake California has ever had.

▲ You can see the San Andreas Fault in the ground. It cuts across California.

66 EYEWITNESS 99

"With boys my own age, I wandered as far as I dared to explore some destruction sites and get a view of local fires. In some places, there were gaps in the ground. Some were about one foot to five feet [30-150 centimetres] wide, narrowing towards the inner earth."

Comments by DeWitt C. Baldwin,
San Francisco, 1906

The 1906 earthquake

A massive earthquake hit San Francisco on 18 April 1906. It measured 8.3 on the Richter scale. In San Francisco, 700 people died, and more than 28,000 buildings were ruined. People saw the ground heaving up and down, trees snapping in two, and landslides. About 300,000 people were made homeless by the disaster.

This map shows where the 1906 earthquake happened. ▼

What we learned

The main lesson was about building methods. Buildings on top of solid rock survived better than those on soft ground. Wooden buildings were less likely to fall down than those made of brick or stone.

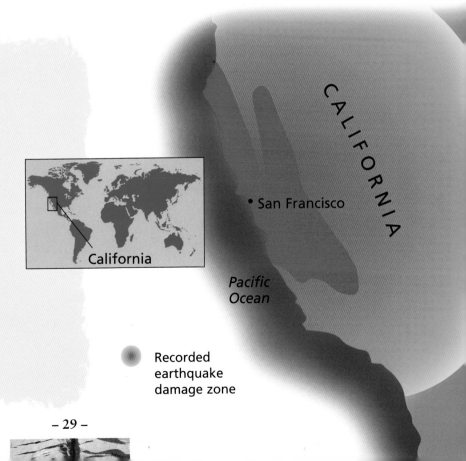

CALIFORNIA

California

• San Francisco

Pacific Ocean

Recorded earthquake damage zone

Other Famous Earthquakes

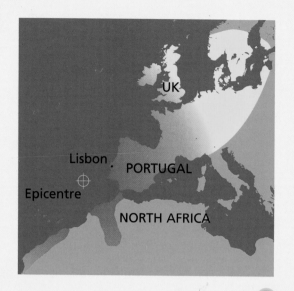

◀ 1755 – Lisbon, Portugal (8.7)

This massive undersea earthquake made the ground move in Lisbon. It caused a tsunami, followed by huge fires. It was so powerful that it was felt in Britain and the Caribbean. About 62,000 people were killed.

 Earthquake damage zone

1857 – Naples, Italy (6.5) ▶

This earthquake killed 12,000 people. An engineer called Robert Mallet studied the effects of the earthquake. He worked out that it had erupted from a single focus point, with shock waves passing through the ground.

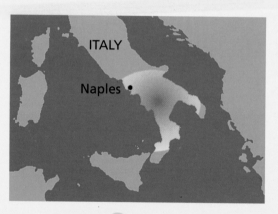

Earthquake damage zone

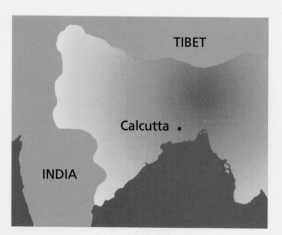

◀ 1897– Assam, India (8.7)

Scientists studied this earthquake and worked out that there were different types of seismic wave.

Earthquake damage zone

1960 – Santiago, Chile (9.3) ▶

This was the most powerful earthquake ever recorded. More than 5,000 people were killed.

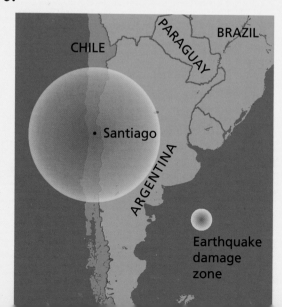

Earthquake damage zone

◀ 1964 – Alaska, USA (8.3-8.6)

This earthquake badly damaged the city of Anchorage. About 125 people died, most of them in the huge tsunami that followed. The tsunami was recorded in Antarctica, on the other side of the world.

Earthquake damage zone

1976 – Tangshan, China (7.5) ▶

More than 240,000 people died in this terrible earthquake. The main shock lasted only twenty seconds, but there were 125 smaller after-shocks.

Earthquake damage zone

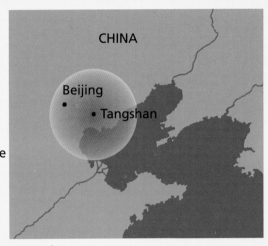

◀ 1989 – Loma Prieta, California USA (7.1)

In this earthquake, 62 people died. Buildings constructed on poor foundations collapsed, and so did roads that were built on two levels.

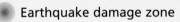 Earthquake damage zone

1999 – Armenia, Colombia, South America (6.3) ▶

More than 2,000 people died in this earthquake. Half of the town was flattened, and 250,000 people lost their homes. The local rescue teams had little equipment or experience. International teams did not get there until two days later.

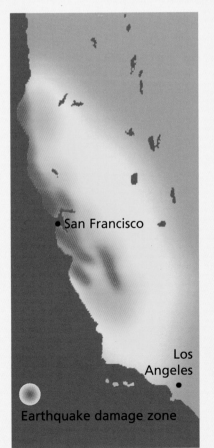

Earthquake damage zone

Tsunamis

Some earthquakes occur underneath the ocean floor. The seismic waves sent out by the earthquake shake the ocean floor and then the water above it. This can create huge waves, which are called tsunamis.

In the open ocean, a tsunami moves very fast – up to 1,000 kilometres an hour. But the wave is small, perhaps only 30 centimetres high. As the tsunami reaches shallow water near to land, it slows down. It becomes a giant wave, up to 30 metres high, which crashes into the coast.

A tsunami sends an energy wave across the ocean. As the sea becomes less deep towards the coast, the tsunami waves grow higher. ▼

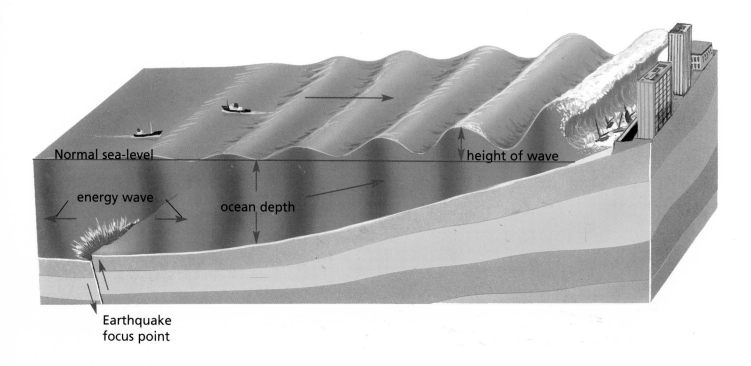

Normal sea-level

energy wave

ocean depth

height of wave

Earthquake focus point

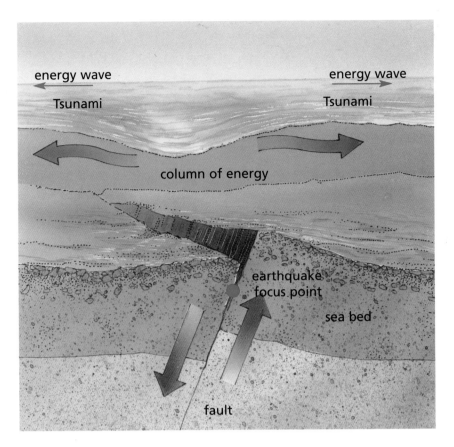

energy wave

Tsunami

energy wave

Tsunami

column of energy

earthquake
focus point

sea bed

fault

▲ How an undersea earthquake starts a tsunami.

Tsunamis in the Pacific Ocean

Nearly all dangerous tsunamis occur in the Pacific Ocean. This is because of the tectonic plates moving underneath it (see pages 12 and13). A big tsunami can sweep across the Pacific Ocean in about 24 hours. It is most dangerous within 400 kilometres of its starting point. Inside this area, the wave will reach coastlines in less than 30 minutes. There is little time to move people to safety.

A tsunami reached Lisbon in Portugal in 1755. ▼

During the twentieth century, 43 small tsunamis occurred in the Mediterranean area. Only two big tsunamis are known to have hit Europe. In 1530 BC, a tsunami destroyed towns on the island of Crete and battered Mediterranean coasts. In 1755, the Lisbon earthquake caused a huge tsunami.

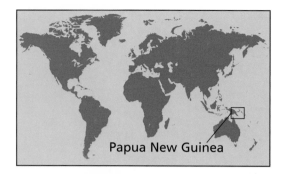

Papua New Guinea

Papua New Guinea

On 17 July 1998, a tsunami hit the town of Sandaun in Papua New Guinea, near Australia. More than 2,500 died, the largest number killed by a tsunami in the twentieth century. Researchers worked out that the tsunami had reached Sandaun less than four minutes after people had felt the first earthquake tremor. There had been no time for people to escape to safety.

Landslide

The earthquake measured 7.7 on the Richter scale. It was not strong enough to cause a huge tsunami. But there was also an undersea landslide. This had made the waves higher and more powerful.

NEWS REPORT

Rescue workers believe that up to 3,000 people were swept to their deaths when three giant tidal waves struck.

Adapted from an AFP press agency report, July 1998

15
10
5
0 metres

◀ The tsunami was 15 metres high at the coast and swept over a kilometre inland.

DID YOU KNOW?

Why tsunamis are killer waves:

● The wave can kill people and damage buildings.

● A tsunami sucks in objects. These things smash into other objects the tsunami has picked up.

Gerry Monana by the ruins of her village in Papua New Guinea, 1998. She is holding a kitten she has rescued. ▼

Rescue and Relief Work

The first thing to do after an earthquake is to rescue people who are trapped under collapsed buildings. This has to be done immediately. In two to six hours, only half of them will still be alive.

International rescue

The International Rescue Corps (IRC) helps out in emergencies all over the world. The IRC carries medicine, food and other supplies, and radio equipment. The team has sniffer dogs and infra-red cameras to help find survivors. The IRC volunteers are ready for action 24 hours a day.

8. Start rebuilding.

1. Check damage.

2. Rescue trapped people.

3. Give emergency treatment.

4. Work out what survivors need.

5. Give emergency food, water and shelter.

6. Knock down dangerous buildings.

7. People go back to work.

▲ The ideal plan after an earthquake.

Sniffer dogs can smell where there is a person trapped inside a collapsed building. ▶

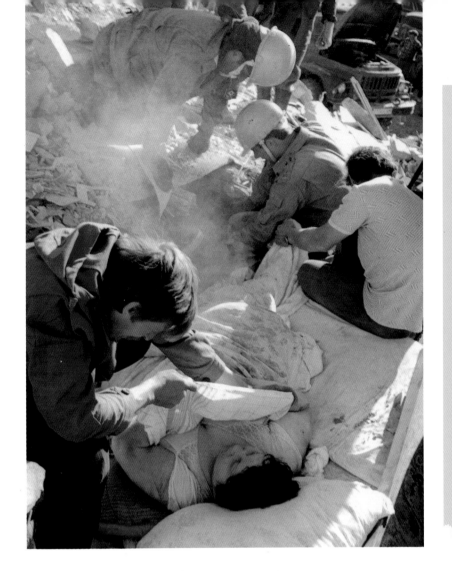

▲ A woman is freed from the rubble after the earthquake in Neftegorsk in Russia, in May 1995.

Medical help

Many people are injured in an earthquake. All rescue workers have some medical training and basic life-saving equipment. But there are not usually enough supplies to help everyone. An emergency system called triage is used to decide who needs to be treated straight away, and who can wait to see a doctor. If the hospitals have been hit by the earthquake, people are treated in temporary medical centres.

66 EYEWITNESS 99

"We don't have enough needles, antibiotics, basic medicines. If we don't receive immediate help, we simply won't be able to cope."

An appeal by Gloria Cardenas, nurse, in Colombia, January 1999

NEWS REPORT

Last week an earthquake killed up to 5,000 people in northern Afghanistan. Ninety-five villages were hit and thousands needed help. The international rescue team had plenty of supplies. But they couldn't get to the survivors. Rain and hail stopped the planes and helicopters from going to the disaster area. "The problem isn't money – it's the weather," said Rupert Colville of the United Nations.

Adapted from *Newsweek* magazine,
15 June 1998

Relief work

After rescuing people from the earthquake, there are new problems to deal with. It is important to stop diseases from spreading, and to find shelter for the people who have lost their homes.

Disease

Diseases can kill as many people as the earthquake itself. Keeping the water supply clean helps to stop diseases from spreading. After the tsunami in Papua New Guinea in 1998, people buried the dead quickly so that their bodies did not poison the drinking water and cause disease.

Shelter

After an earthquake, people who have lost their homes need somewhere to stay. All these kinds of shelter may be used: hotels, holiday homes, schools, offices, ships, trains and buses. Tents are also useful and sometimes shelters are made from plastic sheeting.

◀ A shelter made from rubble after the Mexico earthquake of 1985.

DID YOU KNOW ?

Other countries help towards rebuilding work in a poor country hit by an earthquake. But the country itself pays up to 80 per cent of the cost.

Countries that can afford it may put up prefabricated buildings. They can be connected to electricity, gas and water supplies.

Rebuilding

When an earthquake happens in a poor country, there is little money for new homes. So emergency housing has to be cheap and simple. After earthquakes in Peru and Nicaragua, houses were built from sandbags filled with cement-mix, with metal bars to help hold them up.

A whole town made from temporary buildings, built after the Armenian earthquake of 1988. ▼

Preparing for Earthquakes

Seismologists are always looking for better ways of predicting earthquakes so that they can warn people. These methods do not always work, so people in earthquake zones need to be prepared.

Predicting earthquakes

In 1975, seismologists noticed that water levels were changing in the wells around the city of Haicheng, north-east China. Around a million people were moved from their homes. That evening, an earthquake measuring 7.4 on the Richter scale struck, and 1,328 people died. Without the warning, many more people would have been killed.

Seismic stations

In many earthquake zones, alarm systems are used. In Japan, the railway lines for the Bullet Train have seismic stations every 20 kilometres. These detect movement in the ground. If the ground starts to move, the alarm system switches off the power to the railway lines.

▲ The Japanese Bullet Train travels at 240 kilometres an hour.

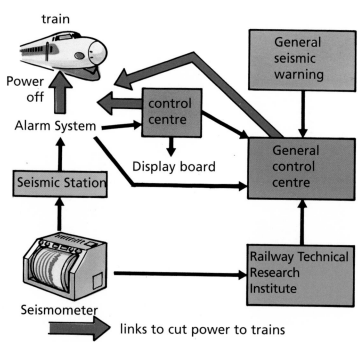

▲ The alarm system for the Bullet Train.

WAYS TO PREDICT EARTHQUAKES

Scientists check for changes in the Earth to help them to predict earthquakes.

1. Underground water

The amounts of minerals and gases in water under the ground can change before an earthquake. Scientists take samples of the water and check them.

2. The tides

Before a big earthquake, rocks may move. If the movements are underwater near the coast, the tides may become higher or lower.

3. Changes in rocks

Rocks are under great stress before an earthquake. The changes alter the magnetic field around them. Scientists can use a magnetometer to measure the changes in the magnetic field.

▲ In California, laser beams are aimed at reflectors across fault lines. If the amount of time it takes for the beams to reach the reflectors changes, the ground has moved.

66 *EYEWITNESS* 99

'Just before the Kobe earthquake, strange things happened. The air conditioner worked on its own without the remote control. The day before the earthquake, the moon looked very pink. The TV channels kept switching of their own accord.'

A description by Hatsumi Haryama, Kobe, Japan, 1995

Safety measures

It is not always possible to predict earthquakes, so good safety measures are needed to protect people in an emergency.

Buildings can be designed so that they do not fall down in an earthquake (see page 21). Architects designed the Transamerica Building in San Francisco on computer. Before they built it, they tested it using computer simulation to see what would happen in an earthquake.

The Transamerica Building in San Francisco, in the USA. ▼

Computer simulation is also used to work out the best escape routes for people in high-rise buildings during an earthquake.

 DID YOU KNOW ?

After an earthquake, people claim money from insurance companies for loss and damage. As well as the everyday things, claims are made for damaged paintings and historic buildings.

UN safety plan

The United Nations has written a safety plan to help governments, companies and local people to cope with earthquakes. If they follow the plan, there should be less damage and fewer deaths.

This man is testing a model building to see how badly it would be damaged in an earthquake. ▶

The UN safety plan for helping countries to cope after earthquakes. ▼

	TIME AFTER EARTHQUAKE		
	Up to 2 days	**2 to 4 months**	**Up to 12 months**
Protecting people	Give emergency treatment	Rebuild medical centres	Plan emergency food and medical aid
Things to be done	Cut off power supplies and chemical plants	Take away dangerous substances	Store dangerous substances safely
Buildings	Move people from dangerous buildings	Prepare to move people from damaged buildings	Strengthen weak buildings

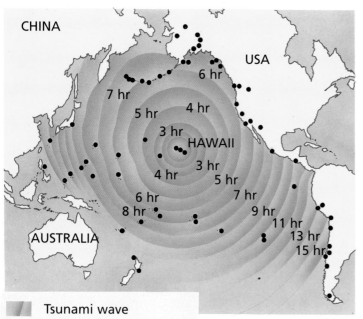

CHINA

USA

6 hr

7 hr

5 hr   4 hr

3 hr

HAWAII

3 hr

4 hr   5 hr

6 hr   7 hr

8 hr   9 hr

AUSTRALIA   11 hr

13 hr

15 hr

Tsunami wave

• Seismic/tide stations

▲ This map shows how long it takes for a tsunami in Hawai'i to travel across the Pacific Ocean.

Tsunami warning

The Pacific Tsunami Warning System warns people in the Pacific countries if a tsunami wave is on the way. Seismic stations and tide stations check for movement in the ground, and changes in the tides. If there is an earthquake that measures more than 6.5 on the Richter scale, an alarm goes off.

Safe from a tsunami

Some of the ways of keeping people safe include:

• planning how to move people away in an emergency

• building on high ground, away from danger, and making buildings stronger

• teaching people about the safety measures.

NEWS REPORT

On 16 August an earthquake that measured 7.8 on the Richter scale happened in the Pacific Ocean near Papua New Guinea. A tsunami warning has been issued for the western Pacific Ocean.

Adapted from Disaster Information Center report, 17 August 1995

◀ Papua New Guinea when hit by a tsunami in 1998.

▲ A Japanese girl taking part in an earthquake drill.

We will probably never be able to stop earthquakes. But scientists will learn more about them so they can give better warnings. Buildings can be made stronger and people can learn what to do in an emergency. All this saves lives when an earthquake strikes.

Glossary

after-effects Things that happen after an earthquake, such as damaged buildings collapsing.

after-shocks Small earthquakes that happen after the main earthquake.

avalanche A mass of snow and ice that falls down the side of a mountain when it is loosened by a jolt - such as an earthquake.

earthquake-proof A building that has been specially made so that it does not fall down in an earthquake is earthquake-proof.

earthquake focus point The place underground where an earthquake starts.

epicentre The point on the surface of the Earth that is right above the focus point of an earthquake.

foundations The base that a building is built on.

landslide A mass of rock and soil falling down a mountain.

marshland Land that is usually quite wet. The ground is soft, so buildings on marshland are likely to fall down in an earthquake.

Mercalli scale A way of measuring how much damage an earthquake causes.

mudflow A mass of mud sliding down the side of a mountain.

predict To try to work out what will happen in the future.

relief Giving help to people after an emergency.

Richter scale A way of measuring the strength of an earthquake.

rubble Pieces of broken stone, concrete and bricks from buildings that have fallen down.

seismic wave A wave of energy made by an earthquake, which travels through the Earth.

simulation A computer model of events to show what would happen in real life.

tremor A small earthquake.

tsunami A huge wave, caused by an underwater earthquake, or by a volcano erupting.

Further Information

BOOKS

The Changing World: Earthquakes and Volcanoes edited by Steve Parker (Belitha, 1996)

Earthquakes by Jane Walker (Watts, 1997)

Earthquakes and Volcanoes by Nicola Barber (Evans, 1998)

Focus on Disaster: Earthquake by Fred Martin (Heinemann, 1998)

The Reader's Digest Children's Book of Earthquakes and Volcanoes by Lin Sutherland (Reader's Digest, 2000)

Restless Earth: Volcanoes and Earthquakes by Terry Jennings (Belitha, 1998)

Wonders of the World: Earthquakes by Neil Morris (Crabtree, 1999)

CD-ROMS

Earth Quest (Dorling Kindersley, 1997)

Violent Earth (Wayland Multimedia, 1997) Includes earthquakes

WEBSITES

There are many sites about earthquakes. Here are just a few:

National Earthquake Information Center: www.geology.usgs.gov/quake.html

Global Earthquake Response Center: www.earthquakes.com

Understanding Earthquakes: www.crustal.ucsb.edu/ics/understanding/

Index

after-effects 6, 7
after-shocks 19, 24, 31
avalanches 6, 22

building design 21, 42

continental drift 10, 11
creepmeter 16

earthquakes in
  Afghanistan 38
  Alaska 5, 23, 31
  Armenia 26, 27, 39
  California, USA 28, 29, 31
  Chile 6, 30, 32
  China 4, 31, 40
  Colombia 4, 6, 19, 31, 37
  India 23, 30
  Italy 7, 30
  Japan 5, 19, 24, 25, 41
  Mexico 18, 23, 38
  Montana, USA 23
  Nicaragua 39
  Peru 22, 39
  Portugal 30, 33
  Russia 18, 37

San Francisco, USA 21, 29
  Sicily 7
  Turkey 4, 20

fault lines 9, 14, 18
(see also San Andreas Fault)

infra-red cameras 19, 36

landslides 6, 22, 23, 29, 34

magnetometer 41
Mercalli scale 17
mud flows 6, 22, 23

Pacific Ocean 13, 33
'Pangaea' 10

rescue 19, 27, 31, 36, 37, 38
Richter scale 6, 17, 22, 23, 24, 25, 26, 29, 34, 40, 44
'Ring of Fire' 12, 13

safety plans 43

San Andreas Fault 9, 14, 20, 28
seismic stations 40, 44
seismic waves 8, 9, 15, 16, 30, 32
  (see also shock waves)
seismologists 16, 28, 40
seismometers 16, 40
shock waves 8, 30
  (see also seismic waves)
sniffer dogs 19, 36
strainmeter 16
subduction 12, 13, 24

tectonic plates 8, 9, 11, 14, 28, 33
tiltmeter 16
tsunamis 6, 7, 24, 30, 31, 32, 33, 34, 35, 37, 38, 44